Codes a

CAMBRIDGE
UNIVERSITY PRESS

Cambridge Reading

General Editors
Richard Brown and Kate Ruttle

Consultant Editor
Jean Glasberg

PUBLISHED BY THE PRESS SYNDICATE OF THE UNIVERSITY OF CAMBRIDGE
The Pitt Building, Trumpington Street, Cambridge CB2 1RP, United Kingdom

CAMBRIDGE UNIVERSITY PRESS
The Edinburgh Building, Cambridge CB2 2RU, United Kingdom
40 West 20th Street, New York, NY 10011-4211, USA
10 Stamford Road, Oakleigh, Melbourne 3166, Australia

Codes and Signals
Text © Phil Gates 1997
Illustrations © Chris Molan 1997 (18 *drum signals* and *smoke signals*; 19; 21*tr*); © Tony Kenyon 1997 (all others)

First published 1997
Reprinted 1998

Printed in the United Kingdom at the University Press, Cambridge

Typeset in Concorde

A catalogue record for this book is available from the British Library

ISBN 0 521 49968 2 paperback

Picture research: Callie Kendall

Acknowledgements
We are grateful to the following for permission to reproduce photographs:

Front cover (© I. Wilson Baker), 5*br* (© Larry Mayer), 22*br* (© I. Wilson Baker), Robert Harding Picture Library; *Back cover,* Collections/Peter Wright; 4, 5 (*traffic lights* and *road sign*), 7, 9, 11 (except *tl*), 12, 13, 14, 15 (*tl, tr, bath taps*), 23, Nigel Luckhurst; 5 (*bar-code scanner*), 11*tl*, 21, Michael Brooke; 5*bl*, 19, Life File (Cliff Threadgold); 15*b*, Sutton Photographic; 16, 17, Trevor Clifford; 22*t*, Hulton Deutsch Collection Limited.

Contents

Codes are words, numbers, pictures and symbols that can have special meanings.

Codes are useful for sending secret messages . . . →

4. 15. 14.'20   20.5. 12. 12
13. 21. 13

Mee tmeatt hega te

← . . . and for keeping things safe.

We use codes every time we make a phonecall or send a letter.

4

← Picture codes are very useful for warning us of danger.

Colour codes give us all sorts of useful information in our lives. →

Some codes can only be → read by a special machine.

← Signals are used to send information from a long distance away.

↓

Secret codes

Codes are very useful for sending secret messages.
Spies use codes so that their enemies cannot read their
messages! *You* can use codes to send secret messages
to your friends that no-one else will understand.

Number code

One of the easiest ways to send a message in a code is
to change all the letters in the alphabet into numbers.

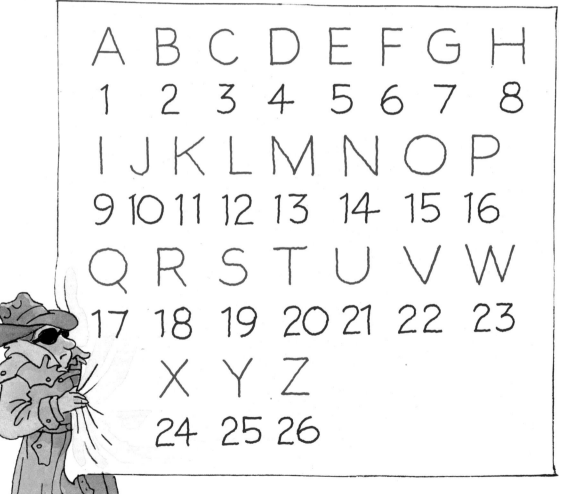

It is called a number code. There are 26 letters in the
alphabet. In this code, 1 means A and 26 means Z.

- This is my name in the number code: 16.8.9.12 7.1.20.5.19
  Can you write *your* name in this number code?

- What does this code message mean?

  4.15 25.15. 21   23.1.14.20 20.15 3.15. 13.5
  20.15 13.25 16.1.18.20. 25?

Make a code book

- Lay some pieces of paper on top of each other.

- Join them together with staples.

- Write a different code on each page.

- You could make up your own secret codes on some of the pages.

- Your friends will need a code book, too, so they can understand the secret messages you write.

Pssst! Here's another secret code idea!

In **reverse number code** the numbers run backwards, like this:

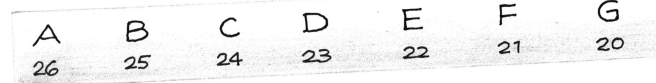

A	B	C	D	E	F	G
26	25	24	23	22	21	20

Finish it and write it in your code book!

Space code

Can you read this message?

It is written in a code that moves the spaces between words. It is called a space code. It puts the spaces in the wrong places so that it is hard to find where one word finishes and another one begins.

If you still can't read the message, turn the page upside down to find the answer!

You are lost in the jungle. What are you going to do?

Try this

Try writing a short message to your friend in space code.

Back-to-front code

← What do you see when you look at some writing in a mirror? In mirrors you see things back to front. Try it!

Here is the alphabet in a mirror. The letter A is on the right! Why do you think this is?

↓

M L K J I H G F E D C B A
Z Y X W V U T S R Q P O N

Try this

You can make a back-to-front code message by writing letters backwards.

Your friends can read it using a mirror.

Symbol codes

You can make codes using pictures or symbols.
Here is an example of a symbol code.

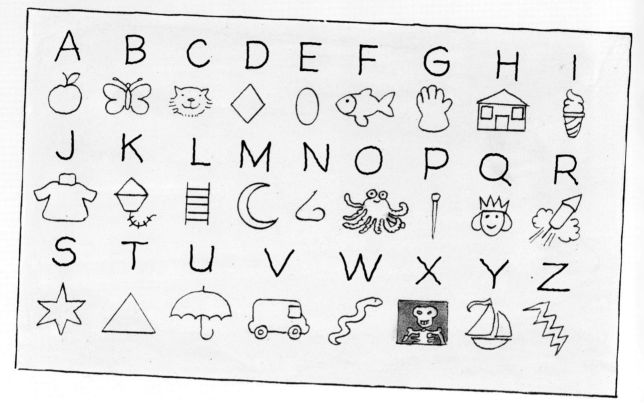

Each different symbol stands for a different letter. So the word 'dog' is written like this:

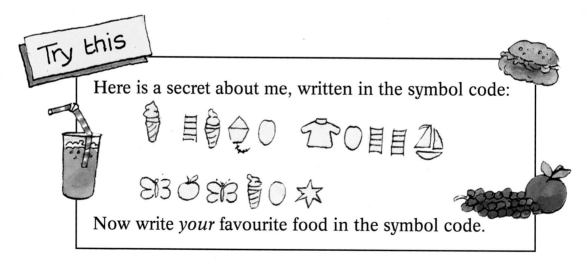

Here is a secret about me, written in the symbol code:

Now write *your* favourite food in the symbol code.

Codes to keep things safe

Secret codes are useful for keeping things safe.

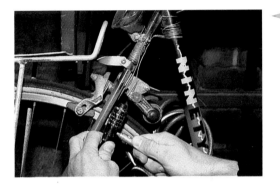

← People can lock their bicycles using a lock with a code. The code is a secret set of numbers that only the owner knows.

Some people keep their money in banks. Some banks have a machine which gives people some of their money when they need it. To use it, they need a special card and a secret code number. →

They put their card in the machine.

Then they type in their secret code number.

The machine gives them their money.

But codes are not only used for keeping things secret. We use codes every day.

◀ When we post a letter, we write a post-code below the address. The post-office can tell where to deliver the letter by looking at the post-code.

Look at this post-code:

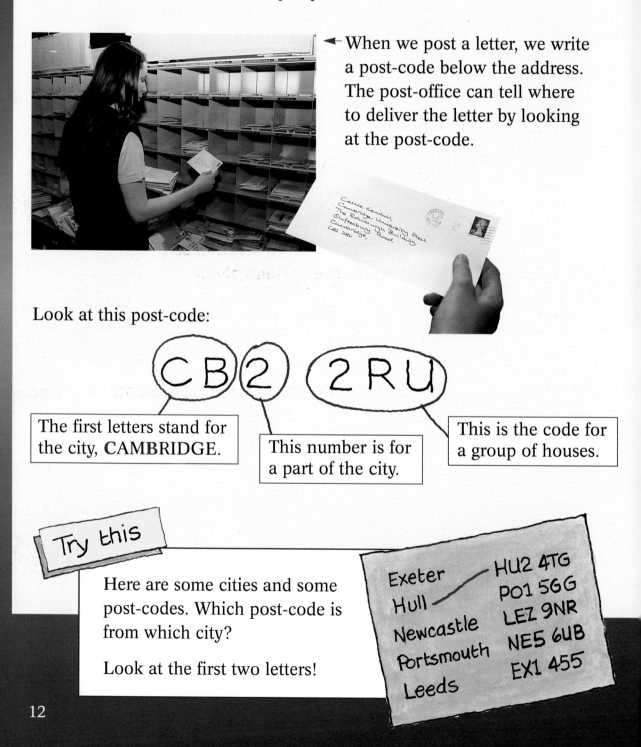

C B 2   2   2 R U

The first letters stand for the city, **CAMBRIDGE**.

This number is for a part of the city.

This is the code for a group of houses.

Try this

Here are some cities and some post-codes. Which post-code is from which city?

Look at the first two letters!

Exeter	HU2 4TG
Hull	PO1 5GG
Newcastle	LEZ 9NR
Portsmouth	NE5 6UB
Leeds	EX1 455

When you want to speak to a friend on the telephone, you dial a telephone number. The number is a kind of code.

Here is a telephone number:

0161 2034300

This is the area code for a town or village.

This is the special number for one person's phone.

Try this

- Find out the area code for your home.
- Do you know the phone number for the police, fire service and ambulance service? The answer is on page 24.

The *phone* book

← Telephone numbers are printed in a telephone directory, which is a kind of code book.

Picture codes that give warnings

Sometimes symbols are used instead of words to give very important information. The ones on this page could save your life!

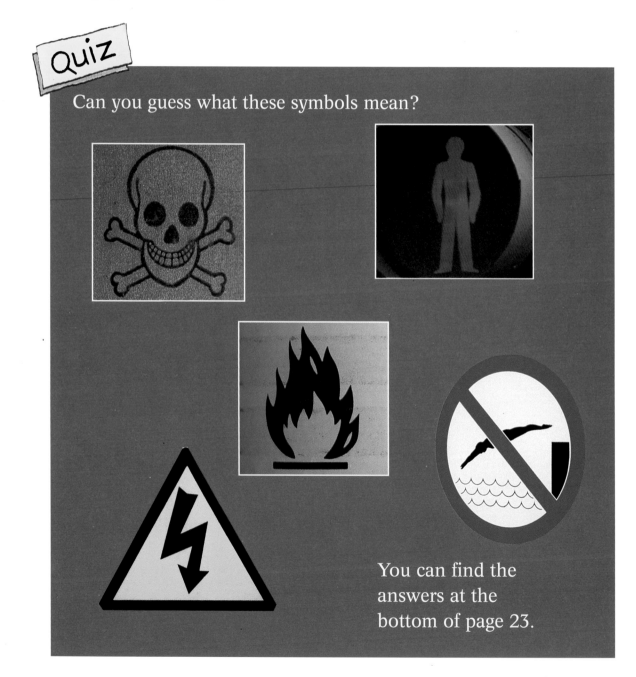

Quiz

Can you guess what these symbols mean?

You can find the answers at the bottom of page 23.

Colour codes

We often use colours as a kind of code.

Traffic lights give messages
to drivers

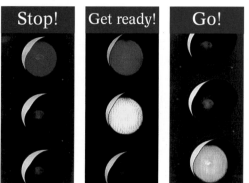

These bottle banks are for recycling
clear, green and brown glass.

Red is for hot water and
blue is for cold water.

Coloured flags are used to give messages
to racing drivers during races.

Slow down and take care!
↓

The track ahead is
slippery!
↘

All drivers must stop!
↓

↓
You have won the race!

Codes that machines can read

Some kinds of codes have to be read
by a special machine.

Can you find the code on the
back of this book?

It is a kind of code called a
bar code.

ISBN 0-521-49968-2

9 780521 499682

Most things that you buy in
large shops have bar codes.

The bar code contains information
about the object and how much it
costs. This information is hidden in
the pattern of black lines.

3

The assistant can read the bar code with a special machine that shines a beam of light across it.

4

iCL

OB 10 MAGIC PENS
                    £1.10

The cash till is like an automatic code book. It can understand the code. It turns the bar code into words and numbers.

5

W.H. SMITH LTD
HARLOW

TELEPHONE NO: 01279 422317
VAT REG NO. 238 554 836

Cashier: SUE C   £
                            1.10

OB 10 MAGIC PENS   1.10

1 BAL DUE   1.10
                            0.00
CASH
CHANGE
3682 009 45 3117 18:53 04JUN9

W.H.Smith

Thankyou For Your Custo

Then it prints out the name and price of each thing you buy.

Long-distance signals

Sometimes we need to give information to people who are a long way away from us. There are different ways to do this. Some were important in the days before telephones and radios were invented.

Drum signals

African villagers used drums to send signals from one village to the next. Different drum beats were used for different signals.

Smoke signals

North American Indian warriors sent secret messages to each other using smoke signals. Smoke can be seen from a long way away. They waved a blanket over a fire to make puffs of smoke. The puffs of smoke were secret messages.

Light signals

Flashes of light are a good way to send long-distance signals.

Soldiers sometimes used to send messages using a special mirror called a heliograph. The mirror reflected the sunlight, and the flashes could be seen from far away.

Lighthouses have powerful electric lights which warn ships that they are close to dangerous rocks. Each lighthouse has its own code, made up of groups of light flashes. Sailors can tell where they are at sea by watching the flashes and using a code book.

Morse code

One of the most famous codes for signalling is Morse code. This code can send long messages or short signals as sounds or as flashes of light.

Morse code is written down as short dots and long dashes, like this:

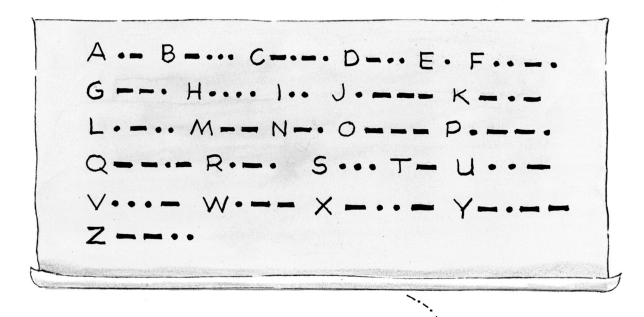

A ·— B —··· C —·—· D —·· E · F ··—·
G ——·· H ···· I ·· J ·——— K —·—
L ·—·· M —— N —· O ——— P ·——·
Q ——·— R ·—· S ··· T — U ··—
V ···— W ·—— X —··— Y —·——
Z ——··

Different sets of dots and dashes are used for each letter. A dot can be a short flash of light from a torch, or a short sound. A dash can be a long flash of light, or a long sound.

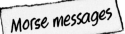

Morse messages

- Can you read the Morse code messages on this page?

- Use a recorder or a whistle to send a message in Morse code to your friend. Blow a long note for a dash, or a short note for a dot. Leave a gap between each letter, and a longer gap between each word.

In wartime, spies and secret agents used torches to send Morse code signals to aeroplanes. Pilots knew where to land to pick up secret agents when they saw the secret code flashing in the darkness.

Today Morse code is sent very quickly over long distances, using telephone lines or radio signals.

SOS

Ships and aircraft send out a special signal when they are in trouble and need help. It is called an SOS, which stands for Save Our Souls.

Can you use a torch to send an SOS in Morse code?

Semaphore

Flags can be used to send signals in a code called Semaphore.

← Sailors sent messages like this between ships before radios were invented. The sailor holds the flags in different positions. Each position stands for a different letter.

A   B   C   D   E   F   G

H   I   J   K   L   M   N

O   P   Q   R   S   T   U

V   W   X   Y   Z

Semaphore is still used today. It → is useful for signalling to aircraft pilots on the noisy deck of an aircraft carrier.

Glossary

alphabet   all the letters that are used to make words

aircraft carrier   a ship which planes can land on and take off from

cash till   a machine that adds up the prices of things that we buy

recycling   using things again instead of throwing them away

spies   people who work secretly to find out secret information (often to help their country during a war)

symbol   a small picture with a special meaning

Warning symbols (page 14)

This can catch fire very easily.

It is dangerous to cross the road when you see the red man.

This is very poisonous. Do not drink or eat it.

Do not touch this or you will get a very bad electric shock.

It is dangerous to dive into the water here.

Index

The telephone number for the police, fire and ambulance service is: **999**